**Put Beginning Readers on the Right Track with
ALL ABOARD READING™**

The All Aboard Reading series is especially designed for beginning readers. Written by noted authors and illustrated in full color, these are books that children really want to read—books to excite their imagination, expand their interests, make them laugh, and support their feelings. With fiction and nonfiction stories that are high interest and curriculum-related, All Aboard Reading books offer something for every young reader. And with four different reading levels, the All Aboard Reading series lets you choose which books are most appropriate for your children and their growing abilities.

Picture Readers
Picture Readers have super-simple texts, with many nouns appearing as rebus pictures. At the end of each book are 24 flash cards—on one side is a rebus picture; on the other side is the written-out word.

Station Stop 1
Station Stop 1 books are best for children who have just begun to read. Simple words and big type make these early reading experiences more comfortable. Picture clues help children to figure out the words on the page. Lots of repetition throughout the text helps children to predict the next word or phrase—an essential step in developing word recognition.

Station Stop 2
Station Stop 2 books are written specifically for children who are reading with help. Short sentences make it easier for early readers to understand what they are reading. Simple plots and simple dialogue help children with reading comprehension.

Station Stop 3
Station Stop 3 books are perfect for children who are reading alone. With longer text and harder words, these books appeal to children who have mastered basic reading skills. More complex stories captivate children who are ready for more challenging books.

In addition to All Aboard Reading books, look for All Aboard Math Readers™ (fiction stories that teach math concepts children are learning in school); All Aboard Science Readers™ (nonfiction books that explore the most fascinating science topics in age-appropriate language); All Aboard Poetry Readers™ (funny, rhyming poems for readers of all levels); and All Aboard Mystery Readers™ (puzzling tales where children piece together evidence with the characters).

All Aboard for happy reading!

GROSSET & DUNLAP
Published by the Penguin Group
Penguin Group (USA) Inc., 375 Hudson Street, New York, New York 10014, USA
Penguin Group (Canada), 90 Eglinton Avenue East, Suite 700,
Toronto, Ontario M4P 2Y3, Canada
(a division of Pearson Penguin Canada Inc.)
Penguin Books Ltd., 80 Strand, London WC2R 0RL, England
Penguin Group Ireland, 25 St. Stephen's Green, Dublin 2, Ireland
(a division of Penguin Books Ltd.)
Penguin Group (Australia), 250 Camberwell Road, Camberwell, Victoria 3124, Australia
(a division of Pearson Australia Group Pty. Ltd.)
Penguin Books India Pvt. Ltd., 11 Community Centre, Panchsheel Park,
New Delhi—110 017, India
Penguin Group (NZ), 67 Apollo Drive, Rosedale, North Shore 0632, New Zealand
(a division of Pearson New Zealand Ltd.)
Penguin Books (South Africa) (Pty.) Ltd., 24 Sturdee Avenue,
Rosebank, Johannesburg 2196, South Africa

Penguin Books Ltd., Registered Offices:
80 Strand, London WC2R 0RL, England

Photo credits: cover: © Jeff Corwin, additional photos: (upper left) © Shattil & Rozinski/Nature
Picture Library, (lower right) © Steven David Miller/Nature Picture Library; page 3: © Doug
Perrine/Nature Picture Library; border (pages 4-48): © Jeff Rotman/Nature Picture Library;
page 4: © Jean-Marc Giboux/Animal Planet; page 5: © Doug Wechsler; page 6: © Paul E. Tessier/
Photodisc/Getty Images; page 7: © Barry Bland/Nature Picture Library; page 8: © James P. Blair/
National Geographic/Getty Images; page 9: © Art Wolfe/The Image Bank/Getty Images;
page 11: © Nancy Nehring/iStock Exclusive/Getty Images; page 12: © Panoramic Images/Getty
Images; page 13: © Bert Gildart; page 15: (top) © Inga Spence/Visuals Unlimited/Getty Images,
(bottom) © John Cornell/Visuals Unlimited/Getty Images; page 16: © Frank Starmer;
page 17: © Nancy Nehring/iStock Exclusive/Getty Images; page 19: © George McCarthy/Nature
Picture Library; pages 20-21: © Lynn M. Stone/Nature Picture Library; page 22: © Bernard
Castelein/Nature Picture Library; page 23: (top) © Shattil & Rozinski/Nature Picture Library,
(bottom) © Tom Vezo/Nature Picture Library; page 24: © Jeff Foott/Discovery Channel Images/
Getty Images; page 26: © Thinkstock/Getty Images; page 27: © Larry Korhnak;
page 29: © Lynn M. Stone/Nature Picture Library; page 31: © Jurgen Freund/Nature Picture
Library; page 32: © Medford Taylor/National Geographic/Getty Images; page 33: © Tim Laman/
National Geographic/Getty Images; page 34: © Lynn M. Stone/Nature Picture Library;
page 35: © Doug Wechsler; page 36: © Adam Britton; page 37: © Joe Raedle/Getty Images;
page 39: © Joe McDonald/Visuals Unlimited/Getty Images; page 41: (top) © Melissa Farlow/National
Geographic/Getty Images, (bottom) © Barry Mansell/Nature Picture Library; page 42: © Stephen
Frink/Photodisc/Getty Images; page 43: (left) © Doug Perrine/Nature Picture Library,
(right) © Georgette Douwma/Nature Picture Library; page 45: (top) © Doug Perrine/Nature Picture
Library, (bottom) © Mike Hill/Photographer's Choice/Getty Images; page 47: © Brandon Cole;
page 48: © Rob Tilley/Nature Picture Library.

Library of Congress Control Number: 2009019094

ISBN 978-0-448-45176-3   10 9 8 7 6 5 4 3 2 1

JEFF CORWIN
THE EXTRAORDINARY EVERGLADES

Grosset & Dunlap

An Imprint of Penguin Group (USA) Inc.

Hi, I'm Jeff Corwin, and I want to take you to one of the most fascinating places in the world—the Florida Everglades! I've loved the Everglades since my first visit there as a child. And every time I've returned, I've discovered something new and exciting.

Some of my favorite animals can be found in the Florida Everglades.

The Everglades is a watery wilderness that covers the southern tip of Florida. In fact, the "glades" is all about water! I should know—I've waded through it, scuba dived under it, and driven an airboat over it!

The wet season in the Everglades lasts from June to September. During this time of year, there's a lot of rain—and afternoon thunderstorms almost every day! All that rain floods the land. That's why people call the Everglades the "River of Grass." During the wet season, a lot of the Everglades looks like one big river!

A hundred years ago, the Everglades covered more than four thousand square miles. That's almost as big as the whole state of Connecticut! But over the years, more and more people moved into the area. They drained the land so they could grow crops, and built highways and homes on it. Today, the Everglades is approximately half the size it once was.

But it's still a wild and wonderful place. You'll see what I mean as we explore all of its different *habitats*. (A habitat is where you find certain types of plants and animals.) So let's get going on our expedition and meet the fantastic animals who call this place home—from alligators to zooplankton, and everything in between!

THE FRESHWATER MARSH

Our first stop is the largest habitat in the Everglades—the freshwater marsh. Because it's so big, this wilderness of water, sun, and wildlife is the heart of the glades. The marsh is actually made up of three smaller habitats: the wet prairie, the sawgrass marsh, and the slough. Each of these habitats is flooded for a different length of time.

The *wet prairie* is flooded for only a short part of the year. That's where we find short, grasslike plants with names such as beaksedges, spikerush, starrush whitetop, and muhly grass.

WET PRAIRIE

The *sawgrass marsh* is flooded for most of the year, and is home to a plant called— you guessed it—sawgrass! Sawgrass isn't actually grass. It's a plant with leaves that *look* like blades of grass. These spiky leaves usually grow up to five feet high, but they can sometimes reach as tall as ten feet. The leaves have sharp teeth along their

SAWGRASS MARSH

edges, just like a wood saw. You sure don't want to roll around in this "grass"!

Running through the freshwater marsh are deep channels called *sloughs*. (Slough is pronounced "slew.") The sloughs are almost always flooded—even in the dry season. Because they don't dry out, these waterways are home to many fish, birds, and other creatures. Plants like water lilies and cow lilies can be seen floating on the surface of the water.

Together, these three marsh habitats are home to an amazing collection of animals. Let's take a closer look at some of my favorites!

SLOUGH

AMERICAN ALLIGATOR

One of the most interesting and important animals in the Everglades is the American alligator.

Guys, this creature is awesome! Alligators in the glades grow to be nearly ten feet long and weigh as much as a thousand pounds! That's a whole lot of gator! The alligator's thick, muscular body is covered with a tough, dark skin. And when it opens its strong jaw, you can see that it has a mouth full of sharp teeth. In fact, an alligator can have up to eighty teeth! It also has a long, extremely powerful tail that it uses to swim and defend itself. You've got to be careful with this creature, no matter what end you're dealing with!

Young alligators eat snails, crayfish, blue crabs, and birds. Larger ones eat turtles, snakes, and mammals such as raccoons and opossums. Large male alligators will even eat small alligators. This is one big, scaly eating machine!

You might think alligators aren't good for anything but eating prey. But every animal is an important part of its habitat. In fact, many of the animals that live in the Everglades depend on the alligator for their survival.

AMERICAN ALLIGATOR

For one thing, baby gators are a big part of the diet of herons, egrets, snakes, raccoons, and largemouth bass. In fact, a female alligator usually lays forty or more eggs at a time, but only one or two will survive to be adults.

Alligators are also important because they dig large holes or ponds in the marsh. These "gator holes" can be as big as fifty feet across. Fish, amphibians, water snakes, wading birds, and many other creatures live and hunt in the gator holes. These ponds are especially important during the dry season. Even when the rest of the marsh dries up, animals can still find water and prey in the ponds.

Since they're so important to life in the Everglades, it's a good thing alligators are protected. In the past, people hunted them for meat and turned their skin into things like wallets, belts, and shoes. That's why they started to disappear. It was almost, "See you later, alligator!" But thanks to protection and conservation, they've made a comeback. That's good news for the gators . . . and all the creatures that depend on them.

ALLIGATORS IN A "GATOR HOLE"

SNAIL KITE and APPLE SNAIL

Compared to an alligator, an apple snail may not seem important—unless you're a hawklike bird called a snail kite. That's because the snail kite eats almost nothing but apple snails.

An apple snail is a two-inch-long, dark brown snail that can breathe underwater. But the snail can also breathe air, like us. The apple snail climbs the stem of a plant until it is near the water's surface. Then it pokes a tiny tube, called a siphon, out of the water and breathes in air. It's as if the snail has its own snorkel! But this is when it's most in danger of being caught. The snail kite hovers over the water and plucks the snail from the water when it surfaces.

Years ago, there were lots of snail kites in the Everglades. But today, it's an endangered species. Can you guess why? When people started to drain the marsh for farming, they destroyed the snail's habitat. And because there were fewer apple snails, there were fewer snail kites. These days, we're taking better care of the freshwater marsh. That's good news for the snails and good news for the kites!

SNAIL KITE HOLDING AN APPLE SNAIL

WHO ELSE LIVES IN THE MARSH

The alligator, the apple snail, and the snail kite aren't the only creatures living in the freshwater marsh.

There's the Florida gar—an odd-looking fish with a long snout and a mouth full of sharp, pointy teeth. The gar usually grows to be three feet long and can be mistaken for a small crocodile.

There's also the American white ibis—a beautiful bird with brilliant white feathers

FLORIDA GAR

and a pinkish orange beak. This bird
wades through shallow water using its
long, curved beak to hunt for prey. It
searches through the mud and plants for
its favorite food—
crayfish and small
crabs.

REDBELLY TURTLES

And there's the
Florida redbelly
turtle. This marsh
dweller grows to be
about a foot long and spends most of its
day basking in the Florida sun. Its dome-
shaped shell is so hard, only the largest
gators can crack it! In fact, the redbelly
turtle often lays its eggs in an alligator's
nest. The alligator keeps most predators
away, so the turtle eggs are safe. As if the
alligator didn't do enough for its neighbors
already! Now it's babysitting, too!

THE PINELANDS

Some parts of the Everglades hardly ever flood, or never flood at all. One of these areas is the pinelands. The pinelands is named for its most common plant, a tree called the slash pine. But how did the slash pine get *its* name? From the slash marks that people cut into its trunk to collect sap.

Remember the daily thunderstorms in the Everglades during the wet season? Well, along with the rain, the storms bring lightning that can cause forest fires. These fires, and fires caused by careless people, are bad news.

But fires aren't always bad. In fact, park rangers sometimes start fires in the pinelands on purpose. They call these fires controlled burns. The rangers do this whenever the slash pines are in danger of being crowded out by too many hardwood trees. The fires stop this from happening by killing all the hardwood trees. Why aren't the pines killed, too? Because this fantastic tree has a special bark that protects it from fire.

It's important to keep the pinelands the way they are because many animals call these forests home—including three of the most beautiful creatures in the Everglades.

PINELANDS BURNING

FLORIDA PANTHER ◇◇◇◇◇◇◇ ◆

You can find mountain lions in many parts
of the United States. They're big, gorgeous
cats with light brown fur, white belly fur, and
black markings on their ears and faces. The
Everglades is home to a special mountain
lion called the Florida panther. It can grow to
be seven feet long—about the same as other
mountain lions. But it is has a thinner body
than its cousins in more northerly states.

This beautiful cat hunts mostly at night,
searching for its favorite food—deer and wild
hogs—or other creatures like armadillos,
rabbits, raccoons, rodents, and even small
alligators. When it spots its
dinner, the panther sneaks
up on it slowly and
quietly. Then, when
it's close enough, it
pounces, grabbing

FLORIDA PANTHER

the animal with its claws and teeth.

Even though the panther is Florida's state animal, it's rare to see one. That's because there are fewer than a hundred living in the entire state of Florida. There used to be many more, but their numbers went down as their habitat became smaller. Today, they're an endangered species. Hmm . . . smaller habitat, fewer animals? Are you seeing a pattern, guys?

WHITE-TAILED DEER

The white-tailed deer is a common animal in the pinelands and the marsh, so chances are good you'll see one. But be very quiet and still if you do! The deer has an excellent sense of smell and hearing. If you startle one or it catches your scent, it will raise its tail like a warning flag and run for safety. And the white-tailed deer is fast—it has a top speed of about thirty-five to forty miles per hour!

WHITE-TAILED DEER

RED-SHOULDERED HAWK

Listen! Do you hear that cry? "Keee-ah! Keee-ah! Keee-ah!" That's the call of another really cool pinelands hunter: the red-shouldered hawk. Look carefully and you'll see this beautiful bird sitting in a tree. It's on the lookout for a meal. And pretty much anything will do: insects, crayfish, spiders, snails, amphibians, turtles, snakes, lizards, birds, armadillos, or other small mammals! Boy, the red-shouldered hawk isn't what you'd call a picky eater, is it?

RED-SHOULDERED HAWK

THE HARDWOOD HAMMOCK

Scattered throughout the Everglades are groves of trees called hardwood hammocks. Hammocks grow where the ground is higher and drier than the surrounding marsh. One of the most common hammock trees is the

STRANGLER FIG

Virginia live oak. It's also one of the most *important* trees in this habitat because it feeds many birds and mammals with its sweet acorns. Plus, birds like the red-bellied woodpecker make their homes in the oak.

The strangler fig is one of the more interesting hammock trees. I'll give you one guess how it got its name. The seeds of the fig are spread by birds that eat the tree's fruit. The seeds end up in the bird's droppings and are sometimes "planted" on a branch, high in a tree. When a seed sprouts, it sends its roots all the way down to the ground. The fig tree grows bigger and bigger until its roots and branches surround the first tree. Hidden from sunlight, the first tree dies—another victim of the notorious strangler fig. Officer, arrest that tree!

The strangler fig isn't the only Everglades plant that can grow without soil. Ferns, orchids, and plants called bromeliads also grow this way. The spores from the ferns and the seeds from the orchids and bromeliads are carried by the wind. If they land in the bark of a tree or on a rock, they can still grow. The plants get everything they need to survive from rainwater and debris like bird droppings and bits of dead plants.

CARDINAL BROMELIAD

Bromeliads are called air plants because they dangle in the air from trees and rocks. One of the most common bromeliads in the glades is the cardinal bromeliad, which usually grows on hammock trees. They have long, green leaves—but they also have bright red leaves that look like flowers.

And check this out—there's an unusual bromeliad called a catopsis. Its spiky leaves form a bowl that traps rainwater. The leaves are covered in a slippery, white powder that attracts insects. When insects land on the leaves, they fall into the water, drown, and decay. The plant then feeds on this "soup" of decaying bugs. I guess the catopsis doesn't mind if there's a fly in its soup!

CATOPSIS

EASTERN DIAMONDBACK RATTLESNAKE ◇◇◇◇◇◇◇◇◇◇◇◇◇◇ ◆

The largest *venomous* snake in North America—the eastern diamondback rattlesnake—lives in the hardwood hammock. (A venomous snake uses its fangs to inject a poison called *venom* into its prey.)

The incredible eastern diamondback grows to nearly eight feet in length! That may sound scary, but if you're careful and treat it with the respect it deserves, the eastern diamondback won't hurt you. Just make sure to admire it from a safe distance and never try to touch it. Like most snakes, it would rather be left alone than attack you.

In fact, like all rattlesnakes, the diamondback has a special way of warning you to stay away. On the end of its tail is a rattle made of dead skin. When the diamondback shakes its tail, the rattle makes a loud, clattering noise that means, "Leave me alone!"

The eastern diamondback comes from a fascinating family of snakes called pit vipers. These snakes have two small holes or pits on their snouts that look like nostrils. The holes are actually organs that detect heat. The snakes use them to sense the body heat coming from their prey. That means they can "see" their prey, even on the darkest night.

EASTERN DIAMONDBACK RATTLESNAKE

THE MANGROVE SWAMPS

Where to next on our journey? Between the freshwater marsh and the waters of Florida Bay lie the great mangrove swamps. These swamps are a wet wilderness like the marsh. But unlike the marsh, mangrove swamps are full of *brackish* water. That means a mix of fresh water from the marsh and salt water from the ocean.

These swamps get their name from the mangrove trees that grow there. Very few plants can live in this habitat. Most plants can't survive with their roots underwater because roots need air. And the salt would kill most plants. So how do mangrove trees do it?

The *black* mangrove's roots grow underwater, but the roots send small shoots up to the surface and into the air. Each little shoot is just like an apple snail's breathing tube. Isn't it cool that a snail and a tree breathe the same way? Even cooler, the black mangrove gets rid of salt through special glands in its leaves. Look closely and you may see salt crystals on the leaves. You can even taste it when you lick the leaf! Hmmm. My french fries need salt. Pass the mangrove leaves, please!

BLACK MANGROVE

The *red* mangrove sits above the water on a tangle of stiltlike roots. Part of the root rests above the surface of the water, so the roots don't have any problem "breathing" air. And brackish water isn't a problem because the roots filter out the salt when they take in water.

The mangrove swamp is home to many wonderful creatures, too. Wading birds like herons prowl through the shallow waters,

RED MANGROVE

searching for fish, frogs, shrimp, and other tasty treats. Then there are roseate spoonbills with long bills shaped like—you

guessed it!—spoons. They wave their open bills back and forth through the water, gathering food.

And there's lots of food to be found, because the mangrove swamp is rich with life. When leaves, twigs, and bark fall into the water, they decay. Tiny marine creatures called *zooplankton* feed on the decaying vegetation. Small fish and shrimp feed on the zooplankton. Then larger fish, wading birds, otters, raccoons, and other animals feed on the smaller fish and shrimp. When animals feed on animals that feed on animals that feed on plants . . . it's called the food chain!

AMERICAN CROCODILE

So who eats the big fish? The incredible American crocodile, that's who!

The American crocodile is a large, greenish gray reptile that looks a lot like the alligator. It usually grows to about ten feet long, but can sometimes grow even longer.

How do you tell a crocodile from an alligator? Look at their heads. Seen from above, the alligator's snout is shaped like the letter U. The crocodile's snout is longer, narrower, and shaped like a V.

You might not know it to look at her, but a female crocodile is a very good mother. In fact, this is one of the ways crocodiles and alligators are alike. Female crocodiles and alligators do many of the same things when taking care of their eggs and young. To begin with, the female croc builds a nest from mud and plant material on high ground that won't flood. Then she lays thirty-five to forty eggs in it and covers them with dirt and vegetation. She doesn't sit on them the way birds sit on their eggs. Instead, the plants create heat as they rot.

AMERICAN CROCODILE

After about ninety days, the eggs begin to hatch. As the hatchlings struggle to escape the eggs, they begin to chirp like birds. When the mother crocodile hears this, she gently uncovers the eggs. Then she uses her teeth to help her babies crack the shells. Once they're born, she even carries them to the water . . . in her mouth! Can you imagine hitching a ride in a crocodile's huge mouth? Once the babies are in the water, Mom keeps an eye out and protects them from hungry birds, fish, and mammals. I've even seen baby crocodiles perched on top of their mother's head. You can bet no one's going to bother them there! Sadly, crocodiles can't protect their

BABY AMERICAN CROCODILE
RIDING IN MOTHER'S MOUTH

young from every danger. Years ago, crocodiles began to disappear from the Everglades as more swamps and marshes were drained. They were also hunted for their skins. Like many other animals, the crocodile became an endangered species. Thankfully, the crocodile's habitat in southern Florida is now protected, and this amazing animal is making a comeback. It's no longer endangered, but the crocodile still needs our care and protection.

FLORIDA COTTONMOUTH

The Florida cottonmouth snake makes its home in the wet mangrove swamps. Also known as a water moccasin, this large serpent is often seen swimming. It grows up to three or four feet long and usually eats fish, frogs, mice, and rats. It has even been known to hang out near the nests of birds that eat fish. If a bird drops its catch on the ground, the snake slithers over to scoop it up. I guess the cottonmouth doesn't believe in the five-second rule!

This gorgeous, dark-skinned serpent is venomous and has a dangerous bite that it uses to catch prey. But like the rattlesnake, the cottonmouth would much rather be left alone. If it sees you approaching, it will try to hide by keeping perfectly still. If that doesn't work, it will warn you to stay away. This snake doesn't have a rattle. Instead, it opens its jaws wide and shows you its fangs. That's when you can see how the cottonmouth got its name. The inside of its mouth is bright, cottony white.

FLORIDA COTTONMOUTH

BURMESE PYTHON

Check this out, guys. There's an unusual visitor to the Everglades who has decided to stay, and people aren't very happy about it!

It's the Burmese python, one of the largest snakes in the world. These giants usually grow to be ten feet long, but some reach lengths of over twenty feet! They're normally found in the rain forests of India and Southeast Asia. So how did they get to the Everglades?

People like to keep Burmese pythons as pets. But when your small, baby snake grows to be ten feet long, it can become too much to handle. So a lot of python owners have released them into the swamp.

But that makes for a python-sized problem. The giant snakes eat the food of the animals who already live in the swamp and compete for living space. They also eat wildlife, including deer and alligators. That's why park conservationists are trying to catch the unwanted serpents and remove them from the Everglades. It's a tough job, but this is one visitor who has definitely overstayed its welcome!

ABANDONED
BURMESE PYTHON
ON A FLORIDA ROAD

BURMESE PYTHON

FLORIDA BAY

Well, guys, we've reached Florida Bay—a warm, sparkling habitat that's home to a wonderful collection of animals and plants. Are you ready to explore?

The floor of the bay is covered in sea grass, algae, coral, sponges, and sea stars. Stingrays, eels, sharks, sea turtles, and many kinds of fish glide through this underwater wonderland.

One of my favorites is the barracuda—a sleek hunter that can grow to be six feet

BARRACUDA

long. With a mouthful of needlelike teeth, it's well equipped to catch the fish it hunts. Plus, it can dart through the water at more than thirty miles an hour, capturing its prey before you can say "seafood buffet"! It's too bad so many people think this beautiful creature is a danger to humans. It may look scary, but the barracuda rarely attacks people. As long as we leave them alone, they're more interested in finding their next meal.

LOGGERHEAD SEA TURTLE

SOUTHERN STINGRAYS

BOTTLENOSE DOLPHIN

Florida Bay is home to one of the most beautiful and intelligent animals on the planet: the bottlenose dolphin. But don't be fooled. Even though the bottlenose looks like a fish, it's not. It breathes with its lungs instead of gills—through a blowhole on the top of its head. And dolphin babies are born live, not from eggs. This makes the bottlenose a *mammal*.

You can find this awesome creature swimming through the waters of the bay, searching for small fish and squid. The dolphin finds its prey using sharp eyes and something called *echolocation*. As it swims, the dolphin makes clicking sounds that travel through the water. When the sounds hit a fish, they bounce back to the dolphin. These echoes tell the hunter where to find its meal. Remind you of anything? Humans use radio waves the same way to locate rain clouds and airplanes. We call it *radar*.

Bottlenose dolphins use sound for more than just hunting. They also communicate with other dolphins using different whistles, clicks, and squeaks. Each dolphin has its own special whistle sound. Scientists think this is one of the ways a baby dolphin can find its mother—by listening for her special whistle!

BOTTLENOSE
DOLPHINS

FLORIDA MANATEE

The Florida manatee swims slowly through the rivers and lagoons of Florida Bay, grazing on sea grass and other underwater plants. And believe me, guys, it eats a lot! That's why it's sometimes called a "sea cow." A grown manatee will eat a tenth of its body weight in a single day. For a thousand-pound manatee, that's a hundred pounds of food! How much food would *you* need to eat if you ate a tenth of your weight every day?

Manatees grow to be about ten feet long. They move their large bodies slowly through the water using their flat tails. And they steer with their paddle-shaped front flippers. When they're eating, manatees can stay underwater for as long as five minutes before they have to surface for air. When they're resting, they can stay under for up to twenty minutes!

Sadly, these creatures are often hurt or killed by motorboat propellers. In fact, it's not unusual to see propeller scars on a manatee's back. The scars remind us that this wonderful creature needs our respect and protection.

FLORIDA MANATEES

Well, that's our tour of the Everglades. I hope you had fun! Maybe some day soon you can explore it for real. Imagine how cool it would be to see some of these awesome

AMERICAN PURPLE GALLINULE

creatures in their natural habitat!

The best way to explore this magical place is to visit the national parks located in the Everglades. There's Everglades National Park and Big Cypress National Preserve. These parks protect the habitats and the animals that live there. The parks are also the best places to hike, bike, paddle, and camp.

If you go, I'm sure you'll fall in love with the glades and make many discoveries—just like I did.